Myths of
Ancient
ROME

Brian Innes

RSVP

RAINTREE
STECK-VAUGHN
PUBLISHERS
A Steck-Vaughn Company

Steck-Vaughn Company
First published 2001 by Raintree Steck-Vaughn Publishers, an imprint of Steck-Vaughn Company.
© 2002 Brown Partworks Limited

Library of Congress Cataloging-in-Publication Data

Innes, Brian.
    Myths of ancient Rome / Brian Innes.
        p. cm. -- (Mythic world)
    Includes bibliographical references and index.
    ISBN 0-7398-3192-5
    1. Mythology, Roman--Juvenile literature. [1. Mythology, Roman.] I. Title. II. Series.

BL802 .I55 2001
398.2'0937--dc21

2001019816

Printed and bound in the United States
1 2 3 4 5 6 7 8 9 IP 05 04 03 02 01

Series Consultant: C. Scott Littleton, Professor of Anthropology,
Occidental College, Los Angeles
Volume Author: Brain Innes

for Brown Partworks
Project Editor: Lee Stacy
Editor: Patrick Newman
Designer: Sarah Williams
Picture Researcher: Helen Simm
Cartographer: Mark Walker
Indexer: Kay Ollerenshaw
Managing Editor: Tim Cooke
Design Manager: Lynne Ross
Production Manager: Matt Weyland

for Raintree Steck-Vaughn
Project Editor: Sean Dolan
Production Manager: Richard Johnson

Picture credits

Cover: The Forum: Werner Forman Archive; Statue of Hermes: Ancient Art & Architecture Collection/Ronald Sheridan

AKG London: 7, 33t, 43, Erich Lessing 12, 40, Gilles Mermet 16b, 45t; **Ancient Art & Architecture Collection:** Allan Baton 9t, Ronal Sheridan 16c, 21b, 21t, 28, 32, 37b, 39, Brian Wilson 15; **The Art Archive:** BritishMuseum London 25b, Dagli Orti 41b, 44, Musee des Arts Decoratifs Paris/Dagli Orti 36, Museo Archaeologico Florence/Dagli Orti 8, Museo Capitolino Rome/Dagli Orti 13b, Museo Civico Udine/Dagli Orti 45b, Museo della Citta Romana Rome/Dagli Orti 41t, Museo di Villa Giulia Rome/Dagli Orti 24, National Gallery London/Eileen Tweedy 27, Private Collection 33b; **Corbis:** Archivo Iconografico SA 5, Christie's Images 19, Araldo de Luca 23, 31, Mimmo Jodice 11, 35; **Hulton Getty:** 17; **Hutchison Library:** Trevor Page 29t; **Mary Evans Picture Library:** 13t; **Scala:** Museo della Civilta Romana Rome 25t, 29b; **Werner Forman Archive:** 9b, 37t, Pompeii Museum 20.

Contents

General Introduction

MYTHS ARE THE MIRRORS of humanity. They reflect the inner soul of a culture and try to give profound answers in a seemingly mysterious world. In other words, myths give the relevant culture an understanding of its place in the world and the universe in general. Found in all civilizations, myths sometimes combine fact and fiction and other times are complete fantasy. Regardless of their creative origin, myths are always dramatic.

Every culture has its own myths, yet globally there are common themes and symbols, even across civilizations that had no contact with or awareness of each other. Some of the most common types include those that deal with the creation of the world, the cosmos, or a particular site, like a large mountain or lake. Other myths deal with the origin of humans, or a specific people or civilization, or the heroes or gods who either made the world inhabitable or gave humans something essential, such as the ancient Greek Titan Prometheus, who gave fire, or the Ojibwa hero Wunzh, who was given divine instructions on cultivating corn. There are also myths about the end of the world, death and the afterlife, and the renewal or change of seasons.

The origin of evil and death are also common themes. Examples of such myths are the Biblical Eve eating the forbidden fruit or the ancient Greek story of Pandora opening the sealed box.

Additionally there are flood myths, myths about the sun and the moon, and myths of a peaceful, beautiful place of reward, such as heaven or Elysium, or of punishment, such as hell or Tartarus. Myths also teach important human values, such as courage. In all cases, myths show that the gods and their deeds are outside of ordinary human life and yet essential to it.

In this volume some of the most important ancient Roman myths are presented. Following each myth is an explanation of how the myth was either reflected in or linked to the real life of the ancient Romans. There is also a glossary at the end of the volume to help identify the major mythological and historical characters as well as explain many cultural terms.

ANCIENT ROMAN MYTHOLOGY

The mythologies of most cultures are a mix of newly created stories and myths adapted from neighboring or more ancient cultures. This holds true for Roman mythology. Many of the most popular Roman myths are reworkings of ancient Greek myths, what the Romans called *intrepretatio Graeca*. Also, over time, many myths were revised to give historical credence to the stories and in turn place divine importance on Rome.

According to the Roman scholar Marcus Terentius Varro (116–27 B.C.), the early Romans imagined their gods as formless powers without

Above: *This 1st-century Roman fresco (wall painting) depicts Aeneas having a wound tended to at the fall of Troy. Virgil made Aeneas the hero of his epic poem the* Aeneid *and linked him to the founding of Rome.*

strong personalities. They did, however, link most of them with particular places. For example, the Romans associated Jupiter, the sky god, with oak groves and the tops of hills and dedicated patches of ground struck by lightning to him.

The ancient Romans also attached great importance to the functions of their gods, who between them presided over all aspects of life.

The goddess Vesta, for example, presided over the hearth, the heart of the home.

When the Romans came into contact with Greek culture, in the 6th century B.C., they were so impressed that they began to imagine their gods in human form, like the Greek gods, and to build temples for them, with statues inside. By the 1st century B.C., not only had the Romans added Greek gods, such as Apollo, to their own, but their great writers had identified all their own gods with Greek gods and had adopted Greek myths and heroes wholesale.

In his epic poem the *Aeneid*, Virgil (70–19 B.C.) changed Zeus and his wife, Hera, from the marginally powerful figures depicted by the Greek writer Homer into the more imposing deities of Jupiter and Juno. Ovid (43 B.C.–A.D. 17), meanwhile, managed to gather the many different strands of Greek mythology into one great but entertaining and popular work, the *Metamorphoses*.

The Romans associated themselves with Greek culture to enhance their own prestige. Sometimes, therefore, they adapted Greek myths to link them directly with Rome. For example, according to the historian Livy (59 B.C.–A.D. 17), Hercules — the Greek hero Heracles — once stopped off where Rome was later built to slay a monster that was terrorizing the people there.

Not even the most important original Roman myth, the founding of Rome by Romulus, escaped Greek influence. The Romans attached great importance to this story. Then, in the 3rd century B.C., a story that the hero of Troy, Prince Aeneas, was somehow involved in the founding of Rome became popular. Trouble was, Aeneas was supposed to have lived some 400 years before Romulus. So, in the *Aeneid*, Virgil made Aeneas an ancestor of Romulus — thereby allowing the Romans to celebrate both their mythical Trojan origins and their legendary founder Romulus.

Romulus and Remus

According to legend, Rome was founded by Romulus, one of two twin brothers who were raised by a she-wolf but later fought over who should rule the new settlement.

LEGEND HAS IT THAT when the Greeks burned and destroyed the city of Troy in Asia Minor (roughly present-day Turkey) more than 3,000 years ago, Prince Aeneas of Troy, son of the goddess of love, Venus (Aphrodite to the Greeks), escaped the flames and sailed to the west. After many travels, he and his companions arrived in Italy, on a plain called Latium. The ruler there, Latinus, had foreseen their coming in his dreams and been told that the marriage of his daughter Lavinia to Aeneas would be the beginning of a great and powerful people. The wedding went ahead, and in due course Aeneas's son Ascanius founded a small town, Alba Longa.

One of Ascanius's descendants was Procas, who had two sons, Numitor and Amulius. Numitor was the older of the boys and so was the rightful heir, but Amulius drove his older brother into exile and claimed the throne for himself. To be sure there would be no one to succeed Numitor, Amulius then made Numitor's only child, Rhea Silvia, a Vestal Virgin. A Vestal Virgin was a priestess of the temple of the hearth goddess Vesta (Hestia), and Amulius's decree meant that Rhea Silvia could never marry or have any children.

However, the god Mars (Ares) visited Rhea Silvia secretly, and soon after she gave birth to twin sons. Furious that she had ignored her obligations, Amulius drowned her in the Tiber River, then threw her babies in a basket into the river.

The basket floated downstream and eventually drifted ashore by a fig tree in the shallows at the foot of a hill called the Palatine. The cries of the two babies attracted a she-wolf. The animal saved the twins' lives by suckling them in a cave. Some time later a herdsman called Faustulus found the twins in the woods, took them home to his wife, and brought them up as his own, naming them Romulus and Remus.

The two boys grew up to be strong young men. One day they quarreled with some shepherds, who captured Remus and took him to their master, who was none other than the exiled Numitor. Romulus followed the shepherds and pleaded with Numitor to release his brother. At this, Numitor realized that the brave twins were actually his long-lost grandsons.

With the help of Romulus and Remus, Numitor then killed Amulius and recovered Alba Longa. However, the twins decided to build a

Above: *According to tradition, this famous bronze she-wolf, now in the Capitoline Museum in Rome, was set up on the city's Capitol Hill in 296 B.C., but in fact it is some 200 years older. The Italian sculptor and painter Antonio del Pollaiuolo added the twins Romulus and Remus, suckling the wolf, in the 15th century.*

town of their own, choosing the site where they had been washed ashore in the basket. But which of them was to be the new town's ruler? To answer this question, Romulus climbed to the top of the Palatine Hill, Remus to the top of the nearby Aventine Hill, and both waited for a sign from the gods. The sign came soon enough. Six vultures circled over the Aventine, but twelve appeared above the Palatine. Romulus declared that he was to rule the new town.

While Remus looked on jealously, Romulus began to build the new town on the Palatine. Finally, Remus could stand it no more and contemptuously showed how easy it was to jump over the half-built walls. Angered, Romulus challenged Remus to a fight and killed him with his sword. Romulus was duly crowned king, and the new town was named in his honor. Centuries later, the Romans placed these events at 753 B.C. and calculated their calendar from this date.

The Founding of Rome

No one knows if Romulus, the legendary founder of Rome, ever actually existed, but there is no doubt that the settlement eventually became the base for a powerful and long-lasting civilization.

The story of Romulus and Remus being suckled by a she-wolf is almost certainly a myth, but the Romans believed it. The wolf appears on early Roman coins, and many experts think that the famous bronze sculpture of a she-wolf in a museum in Rome is Etruscan in origin — and it was the Etruscans who ruled Rome for the city's first 250 years.

Some 2,700 years ago, around 700 B.C., the civilization of ancient Greece dominated the eastern half of the Mediterranean. But Greek influence extended westward only as far as the southern tip of Italy. On the south side of the western Mediterranean, the Carthaginians, based in North Africa, were the dominant civilization. The Etruscans occupied the northwestern part of Italy. The Carthaginians and Etruscans had both originally come from the east. These fierce trading rivals were great seafarers who traveled all over the western Mediterranean, and the Carthaginians even ventured out into the Atlantic.

Meanwhile, tribes of peasant farmers had begun to move from central Europe across the Alps, and into Italy. After several centuries a group settled on the southern side of the Tiber River, on a plain that they named Latium: they called themselves Latins. The plain was only some 30–40 miles (48–64 km) wide, which is smaller than most counties in the United States. But the little town founded there, Alba Longa, was to be the birthplace of the Roman empire.

The Etruscans lived north of the Tiber. To obtain iron weapons or tools, Latin farmers took grain or cattle to a trading post on the south bank, where

Above: *The high quality of Etruscan bronze work is evident in this statuette from about 550 B.C.*

shallow water and an island made crossing easy. A strong fort on top of a hill called the Palatine guarded the trading post, and there were small villages on the other six hills nearby. In between, on low marshy ground, lay an open-air market — known as the Forum — and a cemetery.

Around 750 B.C. an Etruscan chieftain crossed the Tiber, captured the fort and Latium, and

Above: *A Roman mosaic depicting peasant farmers plowing with a pair of oxen. The first Latins were peasant farmers.*

Below: *The ruins of the Forum, with the Palatine Hill on the left and the Temple of Vesta on the right.*

destroyed Alba Longa. A new settlement — Rome — arose on the hills around the Forum. For the next 250 years Etruscan kings ruled over the Latins. The Etruscans brought "civilization" — which means "city living" in Latin — to the peasant farmers. They built a huge arched stone sewer to drain off the water from the Forum and raised great buildings, including a handsome temple to the god Jupiter, on the hill called the Capitol. They also brought beautiful pottery from Greece and introduced the horse-drawn chariot — a wonderful bronze Etruscan chariot can be seen in the Metropolitan Museum in New York City.

However, the Etruscan rulers became too greedy for wealth and power, and around 500 B.C. their subjects drove them from Rome and decided that, instead of being ruled by a king, they would elect two consuls, or magistrates, each year to head their government. This was the start of the great Roman republic, which lasted until Augustus became the first emperor of Rome in 27 B.C.

Diana and Actaeon

The gods forbid mere mortals to look at them without permission, so when the hunter Actaeon saw the goddess Diana bathing in a pool she took terrible revenge on him.

IANA (ARTEMIS to the Greeks), the goddess of fertility and hunting, was the daughter of the king of the gods, Jupiter (Zeus), and Latona (Leto), and the twin sister of Apollo. When she was a young child — some say as young as three — she asked her father to grant her eternal virginity.

Accompanied by nymphs, Diana roamed wild places such as forests, mountains, and marshes, where she danced, hunted game with her silver arrows, and guarded young animals from hunters. She also protected girls and pregnant women, and Roman women prayed and made offerings to her in order to conceive and give birth safely. Like her brother, Diana could bring healing but she could also bring disease and death if angered. When a woman died in childbirth people said that Diana had shot her down for offending the goddess in some way.

Diana fiercely protected her nymphs. Once, her father seduced one of them, Callisto, who then gave birth to a boy, Arcas. Diana punished Callisto by turning her into a bear, and when Arcas grew up he unknowingly hunted and killed his own mother.

Diana was equally protective of her own purity and gravely punished any man who dishonored her in any way. One man who offended her was a hunter called Actaeon. His unfortunate story began when he was out hunting in a forest one day with his followers and pack of hounds and saw Diana and her nymphs bathing in a pool. Furious, the goddess looked for her bow, but it was out of reach, so instead she splashed water in the hunter's face.

Instantly, a pair of branching horns sprouted from Actaeon's head, then his neck lengthened, his ears grew points, his hands and feet became hooves, and hair burst through his skin — Diana had turned him into a stag (a male deer). Seeing his own reflection in the pool, Actaeon fled in terror, but his own hounds immediately gave chase — cheered on wildly by his followers, who did not realize the stag was in fact their master.

Actaeon raced desperately through the trees, the baying hounds hot on his heels. He tried to cry out to his followers, "I am Actaeon! Recognize your master!" but no words came forth. The bloodthirsty pack soon caught him and ravenously tore him to pieces in front of his followers.

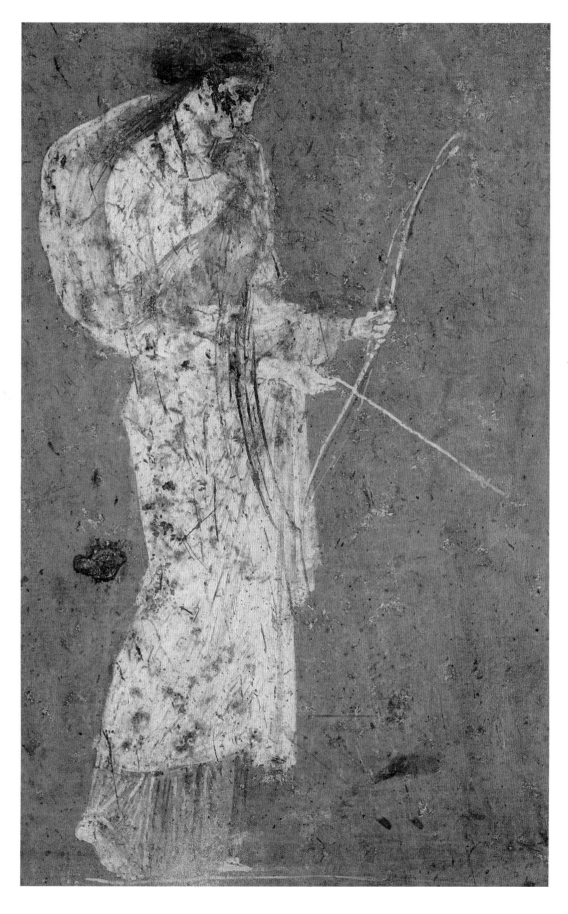

Left: *A fresco — a picture painted on a wall while the plaster is still damp — of the goddess Diana with a bow and arrow, from the ruins of the ancient Roman town of Stabiae, in Italy. Whenever Diana ran out of silver arrows, she simply asked Vulcan (Hephaestus), the god of fire, to forge some more for her.*

Religion and Worship in Ancient Rome

Like the Greeks, the Romans worshiped a host of gods, whom they believed controlled all aspects of human life — for better or worse, according to their pleasure or displeasure.

Originally the Romans had their own gods, headed by Jupiter and the goddess Juno, but from around the 4th century B.C. they adopted Greek gods and identified many of their own gods with Greek ones. For example, they adopted Apollo and identified Jupiter with Zeus, Juno with Hera, and Diana, the goddess who cruelly punished Actaeon for seeing her bathe in a pool, with Artemis.

The Romans held festivals for each god, and they built hundreds of temples where they regularly sought favors, in everything from personal health to success in war, by praying and offering food, wine, and money. Many also had a *lararium*, or shrine, at home, where

Above: *A marble relief, from Rome, of a bull being sacrificed to the god of war, Mars (Ares to the Greeks). It dates from around* A.D. *100.*

they prayed and made daily offerings to statuettes of *lares,* or household gods.

Inside each temple was a statue of its god in human form, while outside was an altar, where priests elected from the nobility often sacrificed animals and studied the *viscera,* or entrails, to determine the will of the god. The entrails were then burned on the altar, and the animal was cooked and eaten.

Roman consuls and emperors tried to find out the will of the gods by consulting special priests called augurs. When a consul or an emperor made a major decision he consulted an augur. The augur then scattered grain in front of his chickens. If they rushed to eat it, the decision was sound.

DIANA WORSHIP

Because Diana was considered to be the protector of slaves, her festival day, in August, was a holiday for slaves. The goddess's main temple in Rome, reputedly built in the 6th century B.C., was on the Aventine Hill. But an even older place of Diana worship was outside Rome, at a site called Nemi on the shore of Alban Lake. Here, custom said

Above: *Alban Lake painted in watercolor in 1818 by the British artist J. M. W. Turner. Here, on the shore at Nemi, Romans worshiped Diana.*

Right: *Isis Fortuna was a personal goddess worshiped at a shrine in the home by many Romans.*

that the priest, called the "rex silvae," had to be a runaway slave who had slain his predecessor in combat after breaking a bough from a sacred tree.

As time went by, many Romans lost interest in their traditional gods and instead adopted "mystery" cults that offered secret rites, sacred truths, and, often, a happy afterlife — something the old gods never did. The cult of the wine god Bacchus came from Greece (where he was called Dionysus), but most cults came from the eastern reaches of the empire.

From Asia Minor (roughly present-day Turkey) came the cult of Cybele, with its ritual of *taurobolium,* in which followers bathed in the blood of a sacrificed bull. From Persia (now Iran) came the cult of Mithraism, which was for men only. The warrior god Mithra slew a mystic bull whose blood gave life. His followers reportedly performed extremely dangerous ceremonies, which helped to make him particularly popular with soldiers. And from Palestine came Christianity, which, following intermittent periods of persecution over nearly four centuries, eventually became the official state religion of Rome in A.D. 380.

The God with Two Faces

A solely Roman god, Janus had two faces, joined back to back, which helped him to see into both the past and the future — and to seduce a beautiful but mischievous nymph.

JANUS WAS THE CUSTODIAN of the universe, the guardian of gates and doors, and the god of all beginnings and endings. He originated all important changes, such as the years and the seasons — the Romans dedicated the first day of the year to him — planting, harvesting, birth, growing up, marriage, and changes of luck. Janus was also responsible for major shifts such as the shift from primitive life to civilization, country to town, and, most importantly to the Romans, peace to war. Almost as powerful as the king of the gods, Jupiter (Zeus to the Greeks), he also controlled all things, and the world moved at his command, Romans said "like a door on its hinges."

The Romans believed that Janus was originally a king, a son of Apollo, who left Greece to become the first king of Italy, founding a town called Janiculum by the Tiber River on the plain of Latium. Here he instituted the worship of the gods and the building of temples, and even became a god himself.

During his reign, Jupiter banished his own father, Saturn (Cronus), from Mt. Olympus, the home of the gods. Saturn took refuge with Janus, shared his kingship, and taught the Latins many skills, including how to farm. His reign with Janus was so popular and peaceful that it became known as the Golden Age.

Janus was one of the gods who guarded Rome. According to legend, he saved the city when the Sabines, a group of invaders from the north, attacked its gates. There was particularly fierce fighting at one gate, and it seemed as if the Sabine forces might gain entry there and capture Rome. But Janus opened a hot spring, flooding the gateway and driving the invaders back.

In religious ceremonies and before wars and other important ventures, Janus was always the first god that the Romans called on, because it was through him that prayers could reach the other gods. Traditionally the Romans kept the gates of his great temple in Rome closed in peacetime and flung them open at the outbreak of war. There were only three short periods in Roman history when the gates remained closed.

Other temples of Janus had a door and three windows on each of their four sides, representing the seasons and months. In them his statues had four faces. Elsewhere they had two: an old face, looking back, and a young one, looking forward.

Above: *The two faces of the Roman god Janus, as depicted on a small silver coin found at a site in Italy. The coin dates from the last quarter of the 3rd century* B.C.

He was also depicted holding a key in his left hand, for opening and closing all things, and a scepter in his right, for controlling all things.

Janus found his two faces useful when he fell in love with Carna, a nymph who lived on the Palatine Hill, the site where Rome was later built. Carna was a flirt who tricked her would-be lovers by leading them to a distant cave, then slipping away. Janus, however, could see her creeping away behind him and caught her. Soon after, he made her a goddess with the power to open and shut doors.

The Roman Calendar

Not only was Julius Caesar (100–44 B.C.) responsible for the greatest change in the history of ancient Rome — from a republic to an empire — but he also ordered the calendar that forms the basis for the one we still use today.

The Romans honored Janus, the god of all beginnings and endings (see page 14), by naming a month after him: *Januarius* (now January).

Ancient peoples found it difficult to work out a calendar, and the Romans were no exception. The early Romans kept close watch on the sun and the moon. From their observations of the sun, they knew that its movements

Above: *Romans kept track of the days and months by marking them with pegs in holes in a clay tablet.*

Left: *A 3rd-century mosaic of Urania, the Roman muse of astronomy, found at the House of Months in Tunisia.*

completed a cycle of 365¼ days, which they designated a year. But they then divided the year into 12 months, based on each new moon rather than the sun.

Besides *Januarius*, the early Romans named three months after gods: *Martius* (now March) after Mars; *Maius* (now May) after Maia; and *Iunius* (now June) after Juno. Because *Martius* came at the start of spring, it was the first month of the calendar year. As for the other months, the early Romans named *Februarius* (now February) after *februs*, a festival of purification. Experts disagree on the naming of *Aprilis* (now April), but it may come from *aperire*, meaning to open, referring to the opening of buds in the spring. The other six months, between *Iunius* and *Januarius*, the early Romans simply numbered: *Quintilis*, meaning the fifth; *Sextilis*, the sixth; *September*, the seventh; *October*, the eighth; *November*, the ninth; and *December*, the tenth.

NEW ORDER

There is a new moon approximately every 29½ days. Twelve cycles of the moon — its waxing and waning from one new moon to the next — total about 355 days. Therefore the early Romans' 12 months totaled less than a year. To make up the shortfall, *Februarius* was meant to be cut short every second year and an extra month called *Mercedinus* or *Intercalaris* inserted. But for various reasons this did not always happen, and by 46 B.C. the Roman calendar was some 90 days behind the seasons — *Martius* was in winter, not spring.

So, on the advice of an astronomer called Sosigenes, Rome's leader, Julius Caesar, decided to reform the calendar. He ordered an extra 90 days to be added to 46 B.C., to bring the calendar

Below: *A marble bust of Julius Caesar. Two years after he rearranged the calendar, Caesar declared himself dictator of Rome for life — so a group of senators, led by Brutus and Cassius, stabbed him to death on the Ides of March.*

into line with the seasons, and decided that future new years would begin with *Januarius*, to honor Janus. He also added a day or two to some months to bring the number of days in a year to 365. To allow for the extra quarter of a day each year, he ordered an extra day to be added to *Februarius* every fourth year (now called a leap year).

The Romans called the middle of each month, when the moon was full, the Ides, and in 44 B.C. a fortune-teller warned Caesar to beware the Ides of *Martius*. On that day, the 15th of *Martius*, Caesar was assassinated. *Quintilis* was then renamed *Julius* (now July) in Caesar's honor. Forty years later *Sextilis* was changed to *Augustus* (now called August) after Caesar's successor, Rome's first emperor.

The "Julian" calendar remained unchanged for 1,600 years. But a year is actually some 11 minutes short of 365¼ days, and by 1582 the calendar was again out of step with the sun — this time by 10 days. That year, Pope Gregory XIII ordered that *Februarius* was not to be given its extra day at the start of each century — unless the century is divisible by 400, as was the case in 2000. This is the calendar we still use today, with the months named much as they were over 2,000 years ago by the Romans.

Ceres and Proserpina

When Pluto, the god of the underworld, took Proserpina, the lovely daughter of Ceres, as his wife, the goddess thought she had lost her child forever — until Jupiter intervened.

CERES (DEMETER to the Greeks) was the goddess of fruitfulness and one of the sisters of the great god Jupiter (Zeus), Neptune (Poseidon), the god of the sea, and Pluto (Hades), the god of the underworld.

Ceres had a beautiful daughter, Proserpina (Persephone). To conceal Proserpina from the eyes of the other gods, Ceres took her to Sicily and hid her there. But one day, as Proserpina was wandering through the fields, picking flowers, Pluto spied her. He rose up out of the earth in his chariot and carried her off to his kingdom below, where he made her his queen.

When Ceres discovered that her daughter was gone, she was heartbroken. She left her home on Mt. Olympus to search the world for Proserpina and neglected her duties. As a result, the earth was no longer fruitful: plants withered and died, the animal herds refused to breed, and famine soon stalked the land.

Jupiter learned from Apollo that his brother had taken Proserpina. He tried to persuade Ceres to return to Olympus and so end the famine, but she refused to take up her duties again until her daughter was restored to her.

In desperation Jupiter ordered Pluto to give up his queen. At first Pluto argued but eventually he agreed that Proserpina could return to the open air. Only then did Jupiter and Ceres discover that Proserpina had eaten pomegranate, the fruit of the dead, at her wedding, meaning that she had made a contract with the underworld forever.

Jupiter arranged a compromise, however. Proserpina would spend six months of each year on earth and six in the underworld. From the start of the time Proserpina was to spend with Ceres — spring — plants would burst forth, ripen, and yield fruits and seeds. Then, when Proserpina returned to the underworld — each fall — the plants would wither until six months later, when Proserpina went back to her mother.

Even though she now saw her daughter for only six months each year, Ceres was overjoyed. She gathered sheaves of wheat and gave them to a Greek prince, telling him how to cultivate the grain. In recognition of this, the Greeks worshiped her in secret ceremonies, first held at a town called Eleusis. Other temples to Ceres were built, and many Romans later made long pilgrimages to Greece to worship her at them.

Left: *In this oil painting by the British artist Dante Gabriel Rossetti (1828–1882), Proserpina holds a ripe pomegranate, the fruit she ate at her wedding to Pluto — so committing herself to the underworld for all eternity.*

Wheat in Ancient Rome

Bread was the staple food of ordinary people in ancient Rome, and the survival of the Roman empire largely depended on a bountiful crop of wheat every year.

Left: *A mill and bakery at Pompeii, the city buried in ash when Mt. Vesuvius erupted in A.D. 79. The three conical structures were for milling flour. Slaves turned the cones with wooden handles to grind grain. The arched structure in the background is an oven for baking.*

So important was wheat to the Romans that they believed it was Ceres (Demeter to the Greeks), the goddess of fruitfulness, who first taught humans how to cultivate it. The poet Juvenal (around A.D. 60–130) famously wrote that the ordinary Roman people longed for only two things: bread and games. The high price of grain — and a consequent shortage of bread — was often the cause of rioting in the streets of Rome.

The Roman army's rations were based on wheat bread. If soldiers did not reach the required standards in training, their ration was changed from wheat to the less appetizing and cheaper barley until they did.

The free people of the Roman state were known as citizens, but most of them did not live in cities or towns. Instead, they worked the land. As the Romans conquered the countries of their neighbors, citizen colonists were given land to cultivate. At first this was sufficient to supply the crops that were needed to feed the population. But the population of Rome was growing fast — it eventually topped one million — and more and more of the land was given over to olive trees, for olive oil, and grape vines, for wine.

When the Romans finally defeated the Carthaginians in 201 B.C. they gained much good grain-growing land in North Africa, southward to the edges of the Sahara Desert. For a long time, Sicily and North Africa were the main sources of wheat and barley for

Right: *Dating from the 2nd or 3rd century A.D., this Roman stone relief from Germany depicts grain being sifted for transport to Rome.*

Below: *This mosaic from Algeria, made in the 1st century B.C., shows a man pruning olive trees. Olive groves and vineyards replaced many wheat fields in North Africa.*

the Roman empire. But there were crises when the crop failed or was insufficient. More grain had to be brought from places such as northern Greece. Eventually, much of Rome's grain was brought from the fertile lands along the Nile River, in Egypt.

DECLINE OF FARMING

Other problems arose. Rich Romans began to buy up the properties of the farmers and bring in prisoners of war as slaves to work these large estates. Soldiers returning from war to their family farms decided that farming was not for them, and went back to their legions. Sometimes they found the farms had already been sold. Families broke up and drifted to Rome, where the emperor had to make free monthly issues of grain to prevent rioting. The gradual disappearance of the farmer-citizens, traditionally the backbone of the army, was ultimately one cause of the collapse of the mighty Roman empire in the 5th century A.D.

The God of Fire

Though crippled from an early age, the fire god Vulcan had massive strength in his arms, which he used to forge metal — and gain revenge on his mother, who cruelly cast him aside.

VULCAN (HEPHAESTUS to the Greeks) was the son of Jupiter (Zeus) and Juno (Hera). Some say that Jupiter and Juno quarreled fiercely one day and that, in her rage, Juno hurled her baby boy off Mt. Olympus, the home of the gods. Vulcan then fell for nine days and nights, finally landing on the island of Lemnos, twisting his feet and dislocating a hip. Others say he was born crippled, so that the gods laughed at him until his mother threw him from the mountain in disgust, whereupon he fell for a day into the sea near the island of Naxos.

Whatever the truth, Thetis and other nymphs rescued Vulcan and cared for him on Lemnos. Here, hidden in a deep grotto, he learned the secret art of metalworking and planned revenge on his mother. Finally, one day he sent her a beautiful golden throne. Delighted, Juno sat on it right away — and immediately was trapped. All the gods tried to free her, but none succeeded.

Jupiter ordered Vulcan to come and release his mother, but he refused to leave his forge. Vulcan's brother Mars (Ares) tried to drag him out, but he drove him off with fire. Bacchus (Dionysus) had more luck. He got Vulcan to drink too much wine and brought him to Olympus slumped over the back of a mule. But Vulcan still refused to free Juno — unless he could marry the beautiful Venus (Aphrodite). Jupiter reluctantly agreed.

On Olympus, Vulcan built wonderful golden palaces for the gods. For himself, he built a dwelling of sparkling bronze, where he set up a forge and made thunderbolts for Jupiter, arrows for Cupid (Eros), Diana (Artemis), and Apollo, and armor for many gods and heroes, including Achilles. His feeble, lame legs supported his big, strong body and arms with great difficulty, so he constructed two golden statues in the shape of living girls. Able to move, like robots, they hurried to his side to support him as he walked.

However, Vulcan preferred underground forges to Olympus. As well as his old forge on Lemnos, he had one under Mt. Aetna, the volcano in Sicily. Here he was helped in his work by the Cyclopes, who were enormous giants, as big as mountains, with a single huge eye that glittered menacingly under a single bushy brow.

Although Vulcan was himself ugly as well as lame, he was forever chasing beautiful goddesses and nymphs. A sea nymph bore him twin sons. The place where they emerged from the earth, at the foot of Aetna, is marked by two pools that are always full of boiling, sulfurous water.

Vulcan guarded his secret art jealously, until one day Prometheus, son of one of the earliest gods, Oceanus, and a champion of mankind, succeeded in stealing fire from him so that human beings could learn how to forge metal.

Above: *This detail from a painting by the Italian artist Pietro da Cortona (1596–1669) depicts Vulcan and his assistants, the one-eyed Cyclopes, hard at work in the fiery heat of his forge, deep inside Mt. Aetna in Sicily.*

Metalwork and Money in Ancient Rome

Advanced metalwork techniques enabled the ancient Romans to conquer armies that were equipped with inferior weapons and to build a vast empire in which Roman coins were the common currency.

The early Latin farmers did not know how to make metal tools and weapons — they had to buy them from the Etruscans. Like the god of fire, Vulcan (Hephaestus to the Greeks), the Etruscans were skilled metalworkers, particularly in gold and bronze, and knew how to extract iron from iron ore. In due course, however, the early Romans discovered the metalmaking secrets of the Etruscans.

Bronze, an alloy of copper and tin, was easily melted in a hot furnace at about 480°C, so that it could be cast in a mold. Iron, though, was difficult to extract from its ore, which had to be heated to around 1,600°C by fanning the flames with bellows. At this temperature the ore formed a spongy lump, which was hammered to drive out the "slag" and force the particles of iron together. The lump was then reheated and hammered into shapes such as plowshares and swords.

After the tool or weapon had been hammered into shape, it was "case-hardened" by thrusting it into a deep bed of glowing charcoal. The surface of the iron absorbed some of the carbon from the charcoal, turning it into a kind of steel.

Above: *Elaborately cast, this Etruscan bronze bowl and stand dates from 750–720 B.C. It probably had a ceremonial purpose.*

When the Romans began to conquer neighboring lands, case-hardened iron weapons were very important to them. The superior quality of Roman weapons was shown dramatically when the Romans decisively defeated the Gauls at the Battle of Addua in northern Italy in 223 B.C. The historian Polybius, who lived in the 2nd century B.C., wrote how the Gauls' inferior swords were "easily bent, and would only give one downward cut. After this the edges were so turned, and the blades so bent, that, unless they had time to straighten them with one foot against the ground, they could not deliver a second blow."

Above: *The iron swords, as shown here, used by the Roman army were much harder than the bronze swords used by the Gauls and did not bend or blunt so readily.*

EARLY MONEY

For several hundred years after the founding of Rome, Greece remained the leading power in the eastern Mediterranean. Greek ships brought trade goods to Rome, tying up at the mouth of the Tiber River. At first, the Romans paid for these goods with grain and cattle — the word "pecuniary," meaning "to do with money," comes from *pecus*, the Latin word for cattle. The Greek merchants, however, paid for their goods with copper and silver coins. Gradually the Romans also began to use rough lumps of bronze — of various weights and shapes — as money, but they did not issue their first coins until around 350 B.C.

Roman Coins

When the Romans first started issuing money, the principal coin was an *as*, a lump of bronze weighing nearly 1 lb (2.2 kg). Twelve smaller coins, called *uncia*, or ounces, made up one *as*. In time, as the *as* lost its value, the Romans introduced other coins, including the alloy *sestertius*, the silver *denarius*, and the gold *aureus*. Initially, coins had images of Rome, animals, gods, or scenes from mythology stamped on one side, but after the republic became an empire, in 27 B.C., they had images of the emperor stamped on them.

Left: *This bronze Roman coin shows the Pharos of Alexandria, the Egyptian lighthouse that was one of the seven wonders of the ancient world.*

Apollo and Daphne

When a lovely maiden chose to be turned into a laurel tree rather than have her purity defiled by Apollo, the god designated a laurel wreath as the highest mark of honor.

ONE DAY, THE GOD APOLLO had a quarrel with Cupid (Eros to the Greeks) over which of them was the greater archer. Apollo scorned the power of Cupid's arrows, saying it was impossible that they could make someone fall in love with anyone Cupid chose, because Cupid was so young and small. In revenge for this grievous insult, Cupid had Vulcan (Hephaestus), the god of fire, fashion him two arrows — one sharp and tipped with gold, the other blunt and tipped with lead — and fired them into the air. The gold-tipped arrow struck Apollo, immediately causing him to fall desperately in love with a beautiful mountain nymph called Daphne — and the lead-tipped arrow struck Daphne, causing her to reject all declarations of love.

Apollo had a rival in Leucippus, a mortal who was also madly in love with Daphne. The daughter of Mother Earth, Gaea, and the Peneus River in Thessaly (a region of Greece), Daphne was a priestess. She and other nymphs devoted to Gaea performed secret rites that were forbidden to men. Leucippus decided to disguise himself as a woman so that he could follow the nymphs,

discover the rites that they performed, and make himself known to Daphne. Dressed as a woman, he soon gained Daphne's confidence. When Apollo found out what Leucippus was doing, he cunningly suggested to the nymphs that they make bathing naked an essential part of their ceremonies, so that everything about their rituals would be pure and undefiled. In doing so, the nymphs discovered that Leucippus was a man, and in fury they tore him to pieces.

Now the field of love was open to Apollo — or so he believed. He found a way to approach Daphne and fervently declared his passion for her. When she immediately rejected him outright, he tried to grab her, but she slipped out of his grasp and ran away in horror. At first, the god was too stunned by Daphne's unexpected reaction even to move. Then he quickly recovered his senses and rushed after her.

As Apollo gained ground on Daphne, she became more and more terrified. Eventually she came to the bank of a river — and there, with nowhere left to run, she called on her mother, Gaea, to save her. The next moment, as she stood on the riverbank shaking with fright, Daphne

Left: *This 15th-century painting by the Italian brothers Antonio and Piero del Pollaiuolo dramatically captures the transformation of the nymph Daphne into a laurel tree as the god Apollo tries to embrace her.*

felt her feet becoming rooted into the ground. Then her flesh began to turn into bark and her arms stretched out as long branches, with her hands and fingers becoming glossy green leaves.

By the time that Apollo caught up with Daphne and threw his arms around her, he found himself embracing a laurel tree. He realized then that he lost the nymph forever. To console himself, he made a wreath of laurel leaves for his head, declaring that from that moment on the laurel was his sacred tree and its leaves the greatest symbol of honor.

The Romans in Battle

By conquering foreign lands, Rome was able to safeguard and feed its ever-growing population, so generals who led Roman armies to victory were hailed as heroes by their emperor.

When the god Apollo tried to embrace the nymph Daphne she turned into a laurel tree, which the god then declared a symbol of honor. A laurel wreath thus became the highest mark of honor, first in Greece, then in Rome. In Rome, when a general returned in triumph the whole city celebrated, and the emperor placed a laurel wreath on his head — for success in battle meant even greater wealth, power, and prestige for Rome.

The Romans began to expand their boundaries soon after the founding of Rome in about 750 B.C. They fiercely fought their way through all of Italy. Much of the land they conquered was given to farmers on condition they served as soldiers whenever needed. Later, other citizens were drawn into the part-time army with the promise

of pay. Soon, the Romans had 300,000 citizen-soldiers. The Roman army was organized in this way until around 100 B.C., when semiprofessional volunteers began to strengthen it. Eventually it became fully professional, with soldiers on a 20-year contract.

Most soldiers were infantrymen called legionaries. The smallest unit was the *contubernium*: eight men who shared a tent and a pack mule. Ten of these units made up a century, headed by a centurion. Six centuries made a cohort, and ten cohorts a legion of almost 5,000 men. Each legion also had a few hundred specialist troops, including archers and cavalrymen.

One reason for the Roman army's success was its superior weaponry. At the start of a battle, each legionary threw a *pilum*, or javelin, which had an

Above: *This gold laurel wreath, found in Greece, dates from the 4th or 5th century B.C. Victorious athletes in Greek games were rewarded with laurel wreaths, and the Romans later honored their conquering heroes in the same way.*

Left: *Detail from Trajan's Column in Rome. Emperor Trajan built this 125-foot (38-m) high edifice in* A.D. *113 to show scenes from his military victories. It was painted when new.*

Below: *A Roman legionary's helmet, shield, and short sword. The shield was long to protect the whole body.*

advancing close together with shields interlocked on all sides and overhead like the protective shell of a tortoise, creating a barrier against most missiles.

Another reason for the Roman army's success was its strict training. Recruits spent weeks learning to fight with wooden swords and shields that were twice the weight of real ones, to strengthen their arms. They also learned to march in time at a strictly measured pace. When on the march, every night they had to build a fortified camp surrounded by a ditch.

Finally, discipline was extremely tough. If soldiers fled the enemy, the punishment could be decimation: picking out every 10th man to be beaten to death by his comrades.

untempered metal shaft that bent on impact, making it difficult to pull out of a body or shield and impossible for the enemy to hurl back. Hand to hand, a legionary fought with a *gladius*, a 20-inch (50-cm), pointed, two-edged stabbing sword that could kill with one thrust into the belly, throat, or face.

Every legion also had specialist engineers who built wooden bridges to cross rivers and huge wooden siege towers, battering rams, and *ballistae* — catapults that hurled rocks — to attack forts and walled cities.

The Romans had superior battle tactics too. The ancient Greeks had attacked in a phalanx, a terrifying but inflexible body of hundreds of men. The Romans attacked in smaller, more flexible groups called *maniples*, each made up of two centuries.

Legionaries could also create a *testudo*, or tortoise — a body of men

The Bloodthirsty God Mars

Early in Roman history, Mars was a god of farming as well as of war — then the Romans identified him with the ferociously bloodthirsty Greek god Ares, exclusively a god of war.

SOME STORIES SAY THAT MARS (Ares) was the son of Jupiter (Zeus) and Juno (Hera), king and queen of the Olympian gods, others that he was born from the union of Juno with a magical herb brought to her by Flora, the goddess of flowers and spring. Whatever the case, Mars grew up to become the god of war and brute courage.

Tall and handsome, yet cruel and vain, Mars liked nothing better than to shed the blood of his opponents in the midst of a fierce battle. Whenever he heard the clash of weapons and yells of war, Mars donned his gleaming helmet, leaped onto his chariot, and gleefully rode into the thick of the fray. Drawn by two fast horses called Fear and Panic, the bloodthirsty god raged about the battlefield, cutting down men with his great sword. Sometimes he slaughtered men on both sides, not caring in the least who won and who lost, so long as he wreaked maximum carnage and spilled as much blood as he could.

The other gods disliked Mars because of his constant thirst for violence, so when he killed one of the many sons of Neptune (Poseidon), the god of the sea, they saw it as the ideal opportunity to punish him. Summoning Mars, the gods put him on trial for murder. But when Mars's own daughter testified that her father had killed Neptune's son because the boy had raped her, the disappointed gods had no choice but to acquit Mars and let him go.

In spite of Mars's great strength and violent rages, other gods and heroes often beat him in combat. During the siege of Troy he fought on the side of the Trojans, while the goddess of war and wisdom, Minerva (Athena), supported the Greeks. Mars was furious when he caught sight of her and struck out at her shield. But she drew back and felled him with a huge stone, saying with a smile, "Fool! Haven't you yet learned how my strength is greater than yours?"

Later, when Mars challenged the mighty Hercules (Heracles), the great hero wounded Mars and he stumbled, groaning, back to Mt. Olympus, the home of the gods. On another occasion, two giants, Otus and Ephialtis, other sons of Neptune, managed to capture Mars and bind him in iron. He was their prisoner for 13 months, until Mercury (Hermes), the messenger of the gods, stealthily released him.

Above: *This sculpture in Caserta in Italy depicts the goddess of love, Venus (left), and her son Cupid (Eros, middle), the god of love, pleading with Mars, who some say fathered Cupid during his affair with Venus.*

Mars constantly fell in love. His most famous affair was with Venus (Aphrodite), the goddess of love, but he had many others and many children, including Romulus, the founder of Rome.

During the reign of Numa Pompilius, who succeeded Romulus as ruler of Rome, Mars let a shield fall from the sky. The Romans believed this was a sign they had the protection of the god. To ensure that nobody would steal the shield, Numa Pompilius had 11 copies made. These were kept under guard in the Temple of Vesta (Hestia), the goddess of the hearth, in the Forum in Rome.

Bloodshed in the Roman Arena

Rome built its empire on bloody conquest. To show their power, emperors held brutal public games in huge arenas called amphitheaters, fueling the bloodlust of the people.

Left: *This amphitheater in Tunisia had wood flooring that covered the arena, but the wood is gone, exposing the stone cells where animal and human victims were kept.*

The Romans celebrated the god of war and courage, Mars (Ares to the Greeks), for his bloodthirstiness. Across the empire, in dozens of amphitheaters, they held frequent games in which people and animals savagely butchered each other.

The biggest amphitheater was the Colosseum, in Rome. Completed in A.D. 80, it held 50,000 spectators, all baying for blood. Emperors held free games here on public holidays. To outdo their predecessors, succeeding emperors held bigger and bloodier games. The carnage reached its peak in A.D. 107, when Trajan presided over the deaths of 10,000 people and as many animals in 120 days of slaughter.

A typical day's killing began mid-morning with games called *venationes*. Animals such as lions, bears, leopards, elephants, and ostriches were let loose on each other, criminals, and prisoners of war — men, women, and children — and were massacred by trained men called *bestiarii*. The beasts came from all over the empire, and killing them in Rome was a clear demonstration of conquest for the people, who could not travel to such exotic places.

Some prisoners were executed, or forced to fight each other to the death — man pitted against man, woman against woman, child against child.

At midday the mangled and mutilated bodies were removed. Perfume was sprinkled on the wealthy spectators in the front rows, to mask the stench of blood and guts, and fresh sand was spread over the bloody floor.

Above: *When a gladiator had an opponent at his mercy, he looked to the emperor who, if people waved white cloths, spared the loser by turning a thumb up; thumb down meant death.*

To a fanfare of horns, trained gladiators — mainly specially chosen prisoners of war, but also a few thrill-seeking citizens — then entered the arena, called out to the emperor, "We who are about to die salute you!" and drew lots to form pairs that fought to the death. Slaves urged on reluctant gladiators with whips and hot irons.

Some gladiators wore a helmet and leg and arm armor and fought with a sword and long, rectangular shield. Others wore no armor and were more mobile. A *retiarius* wielded a trident (forked spear) and a weighted net.

People bet on the gladiators — female fighters were favorite novelties — but few gladiators survived many fights. Those who did might win their freedom and even become celebrities.

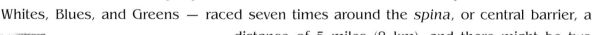

Chariot Racing

Another bloody spectacle Romans bet on was chariot racing, the biggest arena for which, Rome's Circus Maximus, held 250,000 people. Four to twelve chariots from four imperial teams — Reds, Whites, Blues, and Greens — raced seven times around the *spina*, or central barrier, a distance of 5 miles (8 km), and there might be two dozen races in a day. The charioteers were trained slaves who raced for gold. The best might buy their freedom, but many died in collisions, when forced into the wall, or when overturning on the tight curves.

Left: *Races were for four-horse* quadrigae, *like this model, or two-horse* bigae. *Horses had names like* Rapax *(Greedy).*

Mars and Venus

When Mars and Venus became lovers on Mt. Olympus, the home of the gods, they thought their secret was safe — not reckoning on the cunning of Venus's husband, Vulcan.

BORN FROM THE FOAM of the sea, the extraordinarily beautiful goddess of love, Venus (Aphrodite to the Greeks), wore a magic belt that made everyone who saw her fall in love with her. On the orders of Jupiter (Zeus), the king of the gods, she married the god of fire, Vulcan (Hephaestus), who alone knew the secret art of metalworking. But Vulcan was ugly and lame in one leg, and Venus soon found a more exciting lover in his brother Mars (Ares), the god of war and courage. She bore Mars three children — including Cupid (Eros) — without Vulcan suspecting that they were not his own.

Mars ordered his faithful servant Alectryon to keep watch each night so that no one would discover him and Venus together. However, early one morning Alectryon fell asleep at his post. As a result, the lovers stayed too long together and were caught by the rays of the rising sun, which belonged to Apollo. Mars was so furious at this that he immediately turned Alectryon into a rooster, to remind him that it was his job to give warning of the approaching dawn.

But the damage was already done and, very soon, Vulcan learned of his wife's deception from Apollo and planned his revenge. Working secretly in his sweltering forge he made a marvelous net of bronze — a net so fine that it was invisible, yet one so strong that it was unbreakable.

Vulcan hung the net over his wife's bed and told her he was setting out on a journey to the island of Lemnos, where he was raised as a boy and had another forge. Venus and Mars thought this was an ideal chance to be together. But at dawn the next day they woke to find themselves entangled in the net, utterly unable to escape.

Vulcan, of course, had only pretended to go to Lemnos. On finding the two lovers trapped, he gathered them up in the net like fish and hauled them before the other gods for them to laugh at. The gods duly roared with laughter at the sight of Mars and Venus, naked and embarrassed, in the net. Apollo nudged Mercury (Hermes), the messenger of the gods, and asked him if he would willingly take the place of Mars inside the net. Mercury swore that he would, but Jupiter, disgusted by the whole situation, refused to interfere in a quarrel between husband and wife. In the end, Neptune (Poseidon), the god of the sea, secured the release of Mars by undertaking that Mars would pay a fee to Vulcan equal to the value of Venus's wedding gifts. "And if he doesn't," said Neptune, "then I myself will pay, and marry Venus!"

Later, as a punishment, Jupiter made Venus fall in love with Anchises, a prince of Troy. She gave birth to a son, who was Aeneas — and so became the ancestor of the Roman people.

Left: *Mars and Venus in a fresco from Pompeii. Roman artists used brushes made from twigs, reeds, or rushes. For a fresco, they coated a wall in plaster, then painted the background while the plaster was still wet. This made the colors brighter and the painting last longer. They added detail when the background dried.*

Marriage and Family Life in Ancient Rome

Parents in ancient Rome had complete control over the lives of their offspring, arranging their marriages so that they would produce children of their own and so carry on the family line.

The *familia*, or family, was all-important to the Romans, who honored their ancestors and saw it as a duty to marry and have children. The importance of marriage is clear from the tale of the god Vulcan (Hephaestus) avenging the betrayal of his wife Venus (Aphrodite) and her lover Mars (Ares).

At the head of the family was the *paterfamilias*, who wielded *potestas*, or power, over his wife and children. In wealthy families, parents dressed their children like miniature versions of themselves and brought them up to act like adults. Boys usually married between the ages of 15 and 18, girls as young as 13. Their parents chose their partners from families of equal standing. Love was not expected to grow between husband and wife until after marriage. Boys often gave their

Right: *On her wedding day a Roman girl wore a special white dress, with a knot at the waist for luck, and a flammeum, or flame-colored veil. In the ceremony, the* pronuba, *or matron of honor — always a married woman — joined the couple's hands.*

intended bride a gold, silver, or iron ring in the shape of clasped hands, representing the union.

There was no standard wedding ceremony, nor were there any legally binding vows. In poor families the girl might just move in with the boy. There was usually a written contract, though, by which the girl passed from the *manus*, or guardianship, of her father to that of the boy, and the girl's family paid the boy's family a dowry.

In wealthy families, on the day of the wedding, the girl gave up her toys and childhood toga, had her hair done, put on special clothes, and waited at home.

When the boy and his family arrived a pig was sacrificed, and the couple exchanged vows. After the families had shared breakfast and swapped gifts, the boy symbolically dragged the girl from her mother's arms, and everyone set out for his house. Some guests carried torches lit from the girl's hearth, others threw walnuts as symbols of fertility. The girl carried a spindle, symbolizing her new role as a wife.

The boy went on ahead to greet the girl's arrival. When she arrived, the torches were thrown away, and the girl symbolically rubbed the doorway with oil and wreathed it with wool. Because it was considered unlucky for her to trip on entering the boy's home, he often carried her over the threshold.

Left: *A bride-to-be had her hair split into six locks, parted with a bent iron spearhead, and fastened in a cone. In this fresco from Pompeii, Cupid, the god of love, holds up a mirror to a girl having her hair dressed on her wedding day.*

As a wife, the girl's main role was to bear and raise children, but she had much more freedom than before, gaining the status of *matrona*, with responsibility for running the house.

Children and Schooling

Poor Roman children helped their parents at work as soon as they were able to and seldom learned to read or write. In most wealthy families, meanwhile, girls learned only household skills, from their mothers. Education was for boys, who from the age of 7 learned Latin, Greek, and arithmetic at a private school, from sunrise to noon, five days a week. Learning was by memorization and repetition, and pupils were beaten for failing. From the age of 11 they also learned history, literature, and philosophy. Educated slaves called pedagogues, who were usually Greek, sometimes taught the boys at home. In the wealthiest families, boys then learned the art of public speaking, from the age of 14, for a career in law or politics.

Right: *Roman boys wrote on a wax tablet with a bronze stylus, like the examples shown here, and counted on an abacus.*

The Messenger of the Gods

A cunning trickster, Mercury made mischief from the moment he was born — but he so delighted his father, Jupiter, the king of the gods, that Jupiter made him the gods' messenger.

MERCURY (HERMES to the Greeks), son of Jupiter (Zeus) and Maia, a goddess of nature, was born in a cave on Mt. Cyllene in Arcadia. Maia wrapped the baby boy in swaddling clothes, but he wriggled free while she slept and fled to Thessaly (a region of Greece), where his brother, Apollo, grazed cattle. Mercury stole the herd, drove it home — making the cows walk backward and wearing his shoes back to front, so Apollo would not know where they had gone — and hid it in a grotto. Then he killed a tortoise and one of the cows and made a lyre, using the shell of the tortoise as the sound box and the gut of the cow for strings. This done, he sneaked back into the cave and wrapped himself up in his swaddling clothes again.

But an old man had seen what happened and he told Apollo, who dragged the mischievous baby off to Mt. Olympus, the home of the gods, and complained to their father. Jupiter was greatly amused at the tricks of his baby son, but Apollo remained angry until Mercury enchanted him by playing sweet music on his lyre. Mercury then tactfully offered his brother the instrument in exchange for the herd, and Apollo happily agreed. Jupiter was so delighted with Mercury's diplomacy that he made him messenger of the gods, guardian of roads, and protector of travelers, and gave him winged sandals.

Although he had given Apollo his lyre, Mercury still loved music, and one of his own sons, the goat-god Faunus, taught him to make and play reed pipes while he watched over his herd. He also made a flute, which Apollo greatly admired, so he swapped it for the caduceus, or golden staff, that Apollo always carried. For hundreds of years on earth, heralds — the diplomatic messengers of kings and emperors — carried a staff to show they were under divine protection. Mercury's uncle, Pluto (Hades), god of the underworld, would send for him to lay his staff on the eyes of the dying so that they would travel peacefully to the underworld.

As well as being guardian of roads and protector of travelers, Mercury came to represent all kinds of communication and quick-witted ideas, and he was the god of merchants and trade. To honor him, people erected stones along the roads where traders traveled. Later, these became the milestones of more modern times.

Left: *Mercury was originally the Roman god of merchants and traders. But in time the Romans identified him with the Greek god Hermes, and so he also became the messenger of the gods and the protector of travelers. Greek statues usually depicted Hermes wearing a winged hat, as in this case, and winged sandals.*

Music in Ancient Rome

Together with dancing, music was a popular form of light entertainment in ancient Rome. It also played an important role in many religious ceremonies and at public spectacles, such as chariot races and the games at the Colosseum.

The Romans regarded music not as serious art to be appreciated, but as something simply to be enjoyed. This is evident from the story of Mercury (Hermes to the Greeks), the fun-loving messenger of the gods who enjoyed playing the lyre and panpipes, both of which were popular instruments in ancient Rome.

Like many Roman instruments, the lyre, or *kithara*, was Greek in origin. The player plucked its strings like a harp, and its box amplified the sound like an acoustic guitar.

Simple wind instruments such as panpipes were probably the most common kind played in ancient Rome. The traditional instrument of shepherds, panpipes were made from reed or cane whistles of different lengths — the shorter the whistle, the higher the note — and played like a harmonica, or mouth organ. Another popular wind instrument was the bone *tibia*, or pipe, with three or four finger holes to vary the note. Some musicians even played double pipes — a pair of

boxwood, ivory, or silver pipes, one for each hand, that were blown at the same time.

The most complicated wind instrument, if not the most portable one, was the water organ, which was invented in Greece in the 3rd century B.C. A pump forced water into a closed chamber to compress the air inside, then hand-operated valves released

Above: *This mural (wall painting) of an actor and a lyre-player was found at Herculaneum, a town buried in ash when the volcano Mt. Vesuvius erupted in A.D. 79.*

Left: *A modern reconstruction of a Roman lyre. Like the god Mercury (see page 38), the Romans carved the box from the shell of a tortoise and used cow gut for the strings.*

achieve a state of ecstasy or extreme mystical trance. With the cults came instruments such as the *sistrum*, a metal rattle played by devotees of the Egyptian goddess Isis.

Loud instruments were also played at the biggest outdoor events — the chariot races at the Circus Maximus and the gladiatorial games in the arena of the Colosseum. They included tambourines, metal cymbals, and straight bronze horns. Another loud instrument was the *cornu*, a curved horn that looped under one arm and over the back and head. This was also used for signaling in the army.

bursts of air through pipes of varying size to produce different notes, like the bellows of a modern organ.

STROLLING PLAYERS

Like street musicians today, small bands of male musicians sang and played for money in the streets of Rome, often accompanied by female dancers clicking castanets. Wealthy Romans, meanwhile, often hired professional musicians called *virtuosi*, who were often Greek, to entertain themselves and their guests between the many courses at lavish dinner parties. Many *virtuosi* also held concerts and performed in plays at outdoor theaters.

Music and dance were also important parts of worship in some of the many Eastern "mystery" cults that became popular in ancient Rome, their rhythm helping worshipers

Right: *This well-preserved mosaic from Pompeii shows a masked actor playing a tambourine. Roman theaters were outdoor arenas, so instruments played in them had to be loud enough for the whole audience to hear.*

The God of Wine and Revelry

Bacchus, a son of Jupiter, king of the gods, grew up far from his Mediterranean home but eventually returned in triumph, teaching people the secret art of winemaking and gathering an army of faithful followers on his way.

ONE OF THE CHILDREN of the god of war, Mars (Ares to the Greeks), and his lover, the goddess Venus (Aphrodite), was Harmonia, who married Cadmus, founder of Thebes, and bore him four children. Their youngest daughter, Semele, became a great favorite of Jupiter (Zeus). But Jupiter's wife, Juno (Hera), jealous of his lover, disguised herself as Semele's old nurse and persuaded her to beg him to visit her in his godly rather than human form. Jupiter duly arrived surrounded by thunderbolts and lightning — which burned Semele to death.

Semele was pregnant, but Mercury (Hermes), the messenger of the gods, saved her unborn son from the flames. Jupiter then hid him until it was time for him to be born. The boy was Bacchus (Dionysus). To protect him from Juno, Jupiter placed him in the care of Silenus, a son of the goat-god Faunus, on Mt. Nysa in faraway India.

Silenus brought Bacchus up, educated him, and became his faithful follower. Bacchus happily roamed the mountains and forests, an ivy wreath around his head, and learned from Silenus the secret art of turning grapes into wine.

The young Bacchus then decided to return to Greece. On his long journey he led an army of women and men, all playing musical instruments, and rode in a chariot pulled by a lion and a tiger. Everywhere he went people welcomed him, because he taught them how to make wine. Very soon people worshiped him as the god of wine and revelry, and his female followers, called bacchantes, celebrated wild, drunken parties.

When Bacchus reached the Greek islands pirates kidnapped him, thinking he was a king's son and hoping for a rich ransom. But, though they tried to tie him with ropes, the knots instantly came loose. Then the sea around their ship turned into rich wine, a vine sprouted from the mast and tangled the sail, and ivy wound itself round the mast. Finally, Bacchus turned himself into a fierce lion. The terrified pirates leapt into the sea, where they at once turned into dolphins.

Arriving safely on the island of Naxos, Bacchus found Ariadne, daughter of the king of Crete, dumped there by the hero Theseus. On seeing Bacchus she burst into tears, but he soon cheered her up, and they married shortly afterward.

Above: *Bacchus reclines on a couch, his head festooned with grapes fresh from the vine, in this famous oil painting by the Italian artist Caravaggio (around 1571–1610). Bacchus taught people how to grow grapes on the vine, turn grapes into wine, and sweeten wine with honey — sugar was unknown in Europe until the 11th century.*

Food and Drink in Ancient Rome

The Romans are famous for eating and drinking to excess, but only the wealthy few could ever afford to overindulge. Most people in ancient Rome lived on a frugal daily diet.

The image of potbellied Romans lounging drunkenly on couches, holding out goblets for slaves to refill, is a familiar one. Wine was the staple drink, and some Romans worshiped Bacchus (Dionysus to the Greeks), the god of wine and revelry. But occasional bingeing on food and wine was a luxury only the rich could afford.

Typically, Romans ate a light breakfast of bread and cheese at dawn and a light lunch at noon. For the wealthy, lunch might be a little fish or meat, with a few olives, grapes, or figs. Their main meal was dinner, begun in the afternoon to end before sunset, after which their oil lamps gave dim lighting and bed beckoned.

For the well-to-do, dinner was leisurely, sometimes lavish. Dancers, clowns, jugglers, acrobats, musicians, and poets might entertain guests in between the three to ten courses of the meal. Diners dressed in an elegant Greek robe called a *synthesis* and

Above: *Dating from the 1st or 2nd century* B.C., *this Roman mosaic shows three diners reclining with their goblets on a couch, and a musician playing panpipes.*

reclined on couches that held up to three people each and were grouped in threes around low tables. Slaves brought in the food and wine — and fingerbowls, for Romans ate with the fingers of their right hand.

The first course might be olives, peahens' eggs, salad, and shellfish such as oysters. Main courses featured meat such as venison, wild boar, hare, and snails, fish such as sturgeon, and

poultry — anything from songbirds to flamingo, ostrich, or peacock.

Roman cooks — trained slaves — prided themselves on serving exotic and fancy looking dishes. One recipe was for dormice in honey and poppyseeds, while another was for quails and quails' eggs with asparagus. Transportation was slow, so meat, fish, and poultry were rarely fresh. To disguise their taste, rich sauces, herbs, and spices all featured strongly in the dishes. Expensive spices came from Asia, while a highly prized sauce made from sun-dried, salted fish guts came from southern Spain.

In between courses, people who felt full might slip out to a room set aside as a *vomitorium* and deliberately throw up, to make way for more food. A cure for indigestion, meanwhile, was said to be raw cabbage in vinegar.

Above: *This mosaic from Tunisia shows slaves trampling and beating grapes to make wine.*

Right: *Rich Romans kept wine in glass jars and drank it "young" — unlike wine now, its taste did not improve with age.*

Dinner ended with a dessert of fruit, dates, nuts, and honey cakes — washed down, like each course, with yellow, red, white, or even "black" wine. (No one today quite knows what "black" wine was.) Some wines were flavored with honey, while others were spiced. Some were warmed, others iced — slaves fetched ice from mountains in winter. All were diluted with water — drinking wine straight was considered vulgar (though it was polite to belch).

EATING OUT IN ROME

Poor people — the majority — ate much more modest meals of bread, porridge, lentils, and beans, with perhaps a few olives and a little fruit, cheese, and occasionally meat. Most Romans lived in crowded tenements, where ovens were banned for fear of fire, and they had to buy cooked food. Bakeries sold bread, while *thermopolia*, or bars, sold sausages, soup, pastries, pies, and fried fish, as well as beer and wine by the glass.

Roman bread was made from an African wheat called emmer, which provided twice as much protein as modern wheat varieties. In times of hardship, emperors gave the poor free monthly rations of wheat, wine, olive oil (for cooking), and even meat to prevent rioting.

Glossary

Actaeon A hunter who was turned into a stag by **Diana**.

Aeneas Prince of Troy, son of **Venus**, and ancestor of **Romulus** and Remus. He is the central character in **Virgil**'s *Aeneid*.

Alba Longa Ancient Latin village out of which grew Rome.

Apollo God of sunlight, music, healing, and prophecy.

as Ancient Roman coin weighing nearly 1 lb (2.2 kg).

Ascanius Son of **Aeneas** and founder of **Alba Longa**.

augurs Special priests who were consulted by politicians and rulers to read the future and predict the outcome of a decision.

aureus An ancient Roman coin made of gold, originally equal to 25 silver *denarii* (see *denarius*).

Bacchus God of wine.

caduceus Apollo's golden staff which he traded with **Mercury** for a special flute.

Carthaginians (Carthage) North African civilization who ruled much of western Mediterranean, including parts of Italy. For many years they were Rome's main rival.

centurion an officer commanding a century (around 80 soldiers).

Ceres Goddess of agriculture and sister of **Jupiter**.

Circus Maximus Rome's largest arena for chariot racing.

Colosseum The largest amphitheater in ancient Rome, seating some 50,000 spectators.

cornu A large curved horn that looped under one arm and over the back and head of the player.

Cupid God of love.

Cybele A nature goddess.

Daphne A beautiful **nymph** who was loved by **Apollo** but was turned into a laurel tree to escape him.

denarius A Roman coin made of silver, worth 10 bronze *asses* (see *as*).

Diana Goddess of wild animals and the hunt.

Etruscans (Etruria) Pre-Roman civilization who ruled much of Italy, including Rome for 250 years. In the 5th century B.C. they began to lose power to Rome.

Faunus A woodland god, appearing half-man, half-goat.

Flora Goddess of flowers and spring.

Forum Site of Rome's main marketplace and judicial buildings.

fresco A painting made on a freshly plastered wall.

gladius a 20-inch (50-cm), two-edged stabbing sword used by Roman soldiers in battle.

Hercules Mythical hero of super-human strength.

Janus A major Roman god with two faces. Guardian of doors, gates, and beginnings.

Juno Queen of the gods and wife of **Jupiter**.

Jupiter King of the gods.

kithara A large **lyre**, Greek in origin, with a resonating box.

lararium A shrine at home dedicated to a specific god.

lares Small statue of a god placed in a *lararium*.

laurel wreath Symbol of honor and success, worn by generals during processions through Rome following military victories.

lyre A musical instrument similar to a small harp.

Mars God of war.

matrona A married woman whose responsibilities included raising the children and running a household

Mercury Messenger of the gods.

Minerva Goddess of war.

Neptune God of the sea and brother of **Jupiter**.

Numa Pompilius Succeeded **Romulus** as leader of Rome, and received a shield from **Mars**.

nymphs Beautiful female nature spirits of forests and mountains.

Ovid Born in 43 B.C. and died in A.D. 17, author of *Metamorphoses*, which expands and gives a Roman perspective to Greek myths.

Palatine Hill on which **Romulus** first built Rome.

panpipes A wind instrument made from reed or cane whistles of different lengths with the mouth ends bound together in an even row. The shorter the whistle the higher the note.

paterfamilias Male head of a Roman family.

pedagogue Usually a well-educated Greek slave who taught various subjects to his master's sons at home.

Pluto God of the underworld and brother of **Jupiter**.

Proserpina Daughter of **Ceres** and wife of **Pluto**.

retiarius A gladiator who used a trident spear and weighted net.

rex silvae The priest at Nemi, a special shrine to Diana.

Romulus Brother of Remus and mythical founder of Rome.

Saturn Father of **Jupiter** and most other major gods.

sestertius An ancient Roman coin made of alloy, originally worth 2½ bronze *asses* (see *as*).

taurobolium Bathing in sacrificed bull's blood to honor the nature goddess **Cybele**.

thermopolia Bars in ancient Rome that sold beer, wine, and food.

tibia A wind instrument made of hollowed bone with three or four holes to make different notes. It was played like a recorder or clarinet.

Trojans Ancient civilization said by the Romans to be their ancestors. Their destruction is depicted in Homer's *Iliad* and expanded on in **Virgil**'s *Aeneid*.

uncia Small Roman coins worth one-twelfth of an *as*.

Venus Goddess of love.

Vestal Virgin A virgin dedicated to Vesta, goddess of the hearth.

Virgil Born in 70 and died in 19 B.C., poet and author of *Aeneid*, which gives a mythological explanation of the origin Rome, and is based on the Greek epic poems *Iliad* and *Odyssey* by Homer.

virtuosi Professional musicians who performed at dinner parties.

viscera Entrails or internal organs from a sacrificed animal that were studied by priests attempting to read the future from them.

vomitorium A room specially designed for people to vomit in during dinner parties in order to make room for more food to eat.

Vulcan God of fire and volcanoes, and blacksmith to the other gods.

Further Reading & Viewing

BOOKS

Haywood, John. *Spotlights: The Romans*. New York, NY: Oxford University Press, 1996.

Honan, Linda, and Ellen Kosmer. *Spend the Day in Ancient Rome*. New York, NY: John Wiley & Sons, 1998.

James, Simon, et al. *Eyewitness: Ancient Rome*. New York, NY: Dorling Kindersley, 2000.

Mann, Elizabeth. *Wonders of the World: The Roman Colosseum*. Buffalo, NY: Mikaya Publisher, 1998.

Simpson, Judith, et al. *Nature Company Discoveries Library: Ancient Rome*. Alexandria, VA: Time Life Books, 1997.

Stroud, Jonathan. *Sightseers: Ancient Rome*. New York, NY: Larousse Kingfisher Chambers, 2000.

VIDEOS

Ancient Rome: Story of an Empire. Arts & Entertainment Video, 1998.

Ancient Rome: The Glorious Empire. Kultur Video, 1999.

Great Cities of the Ancient World: Rome and Pompeii. Questar Incorporated, 1993.

Just the Facts: Ancient Rome. Goldhil Home Media, 2001.

WEBSITES

LacuCurtius: Into the Roman World. http://www.ukans.edu/history/index/europe/ancient_rome/home.html

Odyssey Online. http://www.emory.edu/CARLOS/ODYSSEY/ROME/homepg.html

Index